TO YOU
LORD

PRAISE TO YOU LORD

PRAYERS OF ST. ANTHONY

EDIZIONI MESSAGGERO PADOVA

ORIGINAL TITLE OF THE BOOK: *A te Signore la lode*
First published in Italy in 1985.
Translated by Claude Jarmak

ISBN 88-7026-687-7

Prayer has always been one of the most basic expressions of a religious person – at all times and in all places.

In the life of the Church, prayer has taken on various forms, according to our personal and communal relationship with God, in a dialogue originating in faith, in conjunction with the sacred Scripture and strengthened by the virtue of charity. Outstanding teachers of the spiritual life have left examples of their prayers, examples wherein we can detect in a concrete form their personal rapport, their intimate relationship with God, who lives in the secret recesses of the heart of a believer.

Among the millions of faithful scattered throughout the earth who are devotees of St. Anthony, very few know him as a teacher of prayer. The Saint's prayers are found, strewn like precious pearls of praise and faith, in only one authentic work which has come down to us from his hand: «Sermones dominicales et festivi». These "Sermones" are actually a manual of theology intended primarily for the spiritual and intellectual formation of his friars.

The 750th anniversary of the death of St. Anthony (1231-1981), celebrated both by the faithful in popular devotion and by the academic world, has given an opportunity to present the Saint as a fervid evangelizer, and the "Sermones" as a source and school of meditation and prayer.

We have chosen selections from his work which are more significant – when his teaching style becomes prayerful. The objective of these Anthonian prayers, therefore, is to experience the faith of the Saint as you read them. We present a meaningful collection which will assist at happy and sad times on our journey of faith toward our eternal goal.

In translating these prayers, we kept two criteria in mind: to follow as far as possible the original text, written at a time and in a style totally different from our ways of expression; second, to render the expressions of the medieval Latin in such a way that they would be understandable to those who would use these excerpts.

Thus, traveling together with Anthony on the road to faith toward the blessed hope, we will find ourselves very close to his heart, and allow ourselves to be guided by the hand of an experienced teacher toward Christ, the center and the aim of our being.

Fr. Livio Poloniato

SAINT ANTHONY PRAYS TO THE TRINITY

1.

We beg you, Unity and Trinity,
that the soul which you have created
may safely flee to you
on that last day of affliction and fire,
when the silver rope will be broken.
Welcome it, that freed
from the snares of evil,
it may come to you with the freedom
and glory of a child of God.
With your help,
one God in three,
who are blessed for all ages. Amen.

(Sermones II/47)

Prayer unites people
to the praises of the
angels.
Altichiero da Zevio,
Coronation of Mary
(detail) Chapel of
St. George.

2.

We humbly beseech you, O God,
to forgive the sins we have committed.
Grant us the grace not to return to evil,
and give us your help
to forgive our brothers from our hearts,
that we may merit the gift of your glory
where you live, who are worthy of praise
for all ages. Amen. Alleluja!

(II/398)

3.

My Lord,
I cannot place the treasure of a sinless life
on the scales of your judgment.
Do not impute this debt to me,
O good God.
Indeed, according to your just judgments, Lord,
I deserve to be condemned
and deprived of my life,
since I did not safeguard the treasure
of my heart and my life
which you have entrusted to my care.

(II/295)

St. Anthony is the exemplar and teacher of Christian life.

St. Anthony Blessing Anonymous, XIV cent. Basilica of St. Anthony.

9

4.

O God, source of all good,
help us to do good,
so we can present to you, who are all good,
an offering of our actions
and hope for a just reward.
Borne by the hands of guardian angels,
may our offering ascend to you,
and may your grace descend on us,
that we may at last arrive at your glory
who are blessed throughout all ages. Amen.

(II/175)

The angel announces
that a savior, Jesus,
has been given.
Altichiero da Zevio,
Nativity (detail)
Chapel of
St. George.

SAINT ANTHONY
PRAYS TO THE FATHER

1.

Father, look at us,
who caused the death of Christ your Son.
As he taught us to do,
we ask in his name
that you give us yourself
because we cannot live without you,
who are blessed and glorious through all ages. Amen.

(I/335)

2.

Do not look at our sins, Father,
but rather at the face of your Christ,
covered with spittle,
disfigured from blows and tears,
he suffered for our transgressions
to reconcile us sinners to you.
He shows you his face
that you may be merciful to us
who were the cause of his passion.
You who are blessed and glorious
through the ages. Amen.

(II/159)

Saints are tokens
of God's goodness
which frees and
saves us.

Girolamo Campagna,
*Resurrection of a
youth* (detail)
Basilica of St.
Anthony.

3.

O, the compassion of divine clemency!
O, the patience of the Father's goodness!
O, the profound and inscrutable mystery of the divine will!
Father, you have seen your only son, equal to you,
bound like a criminal to a pillar
and scourged like a murderer.
How could you have borne this?
We thank you, Holy Father,
because the sufferings and scourges of
your beloved Son
have freed us from the shackles of sin
and from the power of evil.
To you be glory for all ages. Amen.

(I/53)

The Son of God
was shackled like
a criminal
to liberate
man.
Stefano da
Ferrara (?),
The Suffering Christ
Basilica of
St. Anthony.

4.

We thank you, O Holy Father,
for in the midst of a frigid winter
you made springtime blossom for us.
During the winter chill
you have given us a breath of spring:
the birth of your Son, Jesus.
Today the Virgin has given birth to the Son of God,
like blessed earth consecrated by the Father himself,
springing forth nourishment for repentant sinners.
Today the angels sing: «Glory to God in the highest.»
Today silence and peace have returned to the world.

(II/122)

Peace returned
to the world at the
birth of Jesus.
Altichiero da Zevio,
*Adoration of the
Magi* (detail)
Chapel of St.
George.

5.

O house of God,
O gate of heaven,
Confession of sins!
Blessed is he who abides in you.
Blessed is he who passed through you.
Blessed is he who has humbled himself within you.
O, the mercy of God!
O, the excellence of a repentant heart!
He who dwells in eternity
has deigned to come
and live in the humble heart
of a repentant sinner.

(I/78.66)

St. Anthony calls us
to conversion and
reconciliation.
Pietro Annigoni,
*St. Anthony and
Ezzelino* (detail)
Basilica of
St. Anthony.

SAINT ANTHONY PRAYS TO JESUS CHRIST, THE SON

1.

Lord Jesus,
make of us good and fertile soil,
for the reception of the seed of your grace,
and make it yield worthy fruits of penance,
so that with your help
we may merit to live eternally in your glory,
who are blessed throughout all ages. Amen.

(I/37)

Christ the Savior is
the heart of our
faith.
Altichiero da Zevio,
Coronation of Mary
(detail) Chapel of
St. George.

2.

Lord Jesus,
grant that we may ascend the mountain of a holy life
from this valley of tears,
so that, conformed to your Passion,
and well grounded in meekness and mercy,
we may be enveloped by your cloud of light,
and hear the voice full of joy proclaiming:
«Come, beloved of my Father, receive the kingdom
which has been prepared for you
from the beginning of the world.»
To you be honor, glory and power,
majesty and eternity
throughout all ages. Amen.

(I/101)

From their glory in heaven the Saints intercede for the well-being of men.
Filippo da Verona, *St. Anthony appears to Bl. Luke Belludi* (detail) School of the Saint.

3.

Lord Jesus,
do not hide your face from us,
do not draw away from our hearts,
and do not call us into judgment for our sins.
Pour your grace into us,
pardon our faults,
free us from eternal death,
and lead us into your kingdom
where we can see the day of eternity
with Abraham, Isaac and Jacob.
With your help, you who are worthy
of all honor, power, praise
and majesty
throughout all ages. Amen.

(I/183)

The object of
Christian hope is
eternal life.
Filippo da Verona,
*St. Anthony appears
to Luke Belludi*
(detail) School of
the Saint.

4.

We beseech you, blessed Jesus,
to call us with fear and your love
in your church;
guide us to yourself from this place of exile.
Make your home in our souls, our king,
so that we become like little children
whom you so loved on this earth
and can attain eternal bliss
of the holy Jerusalem
to praise, bless and glorify you.
With your help,
who are worthy of glory and honor
throughout all ages. Amen.

(I/204)

5.

Lord Jesus Christ,
pour your grace into us,
so that we may ask and receive from you
the plenitude of true life.
Ask the Father for us
to receive true faith,
to merit a place in eternal life.
With your help,
who are the beginning and end,
worthy of praise, admirable and ineffable,
throughout all ages. Amen.

(I/350-351)

Faith is our guide from the exile of this earth to the eternal beatitude.

Achille Casanova *Madonna with the baby in glory.* Basilica of St. Anthony.

26

6.

Lord Jesus Christ,
may we board the boat of Simon Peter
with the virtue of obedience.
Steer our lives away
from the things of this world
to the heights of contemplation;
help us cast our fishing nets
that we may get a great catch of good works
and attain to you, good and great God,
who reign gloriously through ages. Amen.

(I/503-504)

7.

Lord Jesus Christ,
we beg you to give us love for you and our neighbor,
make us children of light,
defend us from falling into sin,
and from the temptations of the evil one,
that we may deserve to ascend to the
glorious light of your face.
With your help,
who are blessed and glorious
throughout all ages. Amen.

(II/26)

The Lord Jesus
frees men from sin
and from death.

Jacopo Sansovino,
*Resurrection of the
drowned person*
(detail) Basilica
of St. Anthony.

8.

Lord Jesus,
bind us to you and to our neighbor with love;
may our hearts not be turned away from you,
may our souls not be deceived,
nor our talents or minds enticed
by the allurements of sin,
so that we may never distance ourselves
from your love.
Thus may we love our neighbor as ourselves
with strength, wisdom and gentleness.
With your help, you who are blessed
throughout all ages. Amen.

(II/168)

9.

Lord Jesus,
lift us up from worldly cares on the wings of virtue,
clothe us with the innocence of purity,
that we can bear our brothers' frailties
as you did, Lord,
and be worthy of reaching you.
With your help,
you who are blessed from age to age. Amen.

(II/241)

As Christ did, so do the true disciples bear the burden of their brothers' sufferings. Giannantonio Corona, *Arrival of St. Anthony at Padua* (detail) School of the Saint.

10.

Lord Jesus,
may you be loyal to the covenant
which you have ratified with your blood
for your children.
May we not fall prey to the evil one.
May we utter your words with trust.
Do not abandon the souls of your servants
which you have redeemed,
who apart from you have nothing to hope for.
Support us, Lord, with your staff of power
because we are your poor.
Guide us, do not abandon us,
lest we go wrong without you.
Bring us all to the end,
make us perfect as yourself, so that
we may reach you who are the object of all our hope.
Arise, Lord, do not appear to be sleeping,
do not look at our sins, but rather at our repentance,
divide the grain from the chaff,
separate the penitent souls from the evil ones,
for whom you have suffered the judgment of Pilate.
You who are blessed and glorious for all ages. Amen.

(II/102)

Christ has renewed
the covenant
between God
and man with his
sacrifice.

Altichiero da Zevio,
Crucifixion, (detail)
Chapel of
St. George.

11.

Lord Jesus,
take us with Your merciful hand,
and lead us out of the cesspool of sin.
Heal us of lust and greed
by your humility and poverty.
Preserve in us a oneness of spirit
so that we may join you
who with the Father and the Holy Spirit
are three in one Lord.
With your help
who are blessed throughout all ages. Amen.

(II/287)

12.

Lord Jesus Christ,
grant us to approach your feast of the incarnation
with faith and humility,
to celebrate the marriage of penance,
so that, with your help,
we can be present at the joyful celebration
of your celestial glory.
You who are blessed throughout the ages. Amen.

(II/337)

We can attain the glory of heaven with the help of the Lord Jesus.
Giusto de' Menabuoi, *Madonna with Saints* (detail) Basilica of St. Anthony.

13.

Lord Jesus Christ,
by humility, uproot the hypocrisy of our pride,
by poverty, drive out greed,
by patience, shatter our anger,
by the obedience of your passion,
repress our disobedience,
that we may deserve to rejoice always with you.
With your help
who are blessed through all ages. Amen.

(II/321)

14.

Christ the Lord,
we ask you humbly
gather us under the wings of your love,
keep us alive
with the water of remorse,
with the air of contemplation,
with the fire of love,
with the earth of humility,
so that we may be worthy of joining you who are life itself.
With your help,
who are blessed throughout the ages. Amen.

(II/394)

Let us pray that
God may extricate
all evil from our
hearts.
Titian, *Miracle of
the jealous husband*
(detail) School of
the Saint.

15.

O Son of God,
when the last day of our life arrives,
free us from the mockery of the evil one.
Escorted by angels
may we join you in eternal bliss.
With your help
who are blessed throughout the ages. Amen.

(II/468)

16.

Lord Jesus Christ,
may we sing your song of praise,
rejoice only in you,
live modestly,
abandon our worries,
and tell you all our needs,
so that in the refuge of your peace,
we can live in the kingdom of the celestial Jerusalem.
With your help
who are blessed and glorious for eternal ages. Amen.

(II/50)

Following the
example of Christ,
St. Anthony
preached peace and
fraternity among the
people.
Giannantonio
Corona,
*St. Anthony meets
Ezzelino* (detail)
School of the Saint.

17.

Lord Jesus Christ,
may the shepherds of your church
watch over the flock of your faithful worthily,
so that they may successfully reach you,
who are the Pasch of all the saints.
With your help,
who are blessed throughout all ages. Amen.

(I/259)

18.

Sweet Jesus,
is there anything sweeter than you?
The memory of you is more delightful than anything else.
Your name is joy;
it is the true gate of our salvation.
What else are you, Jesus,
if not our Savior?
Be our Redeemer.
Give us the virtues of hope and love,
just as you have given us faith, our primary joy.
May we live and die in them
so we can attain you.
With your help
and through the prayers of your Mother,
you who are blessed throughout the ages. Amen.

(III/112)

The memory of Jesu
sweeter than anythin
else.
Altichiero da Zevio,
Flight to Egypt
(detail) Chapel
of St. George.

19.

O eyes of our loved one,
closed in the sleep of death!
O face,
on whom the angels longed to gaze,
now become pale.
O lips,
which like a honeycomb exuded words of eternal life
now become livid.
O head,
before which the angels trembled,
now hanging limp.
Those hands at whose touch
leprosy was cured,
life was restored,
eyesight was recovered,
devils were put to flight,
bread was multiplied —
are now pierced with nails and
stained with the precious blood!

(III/177)

In Christ crucified
we encounter
the greatest proof
of the love of God.

Pietro Annigoni,
*The
Crucifixion.*
Basilica of
St. Anthony.

20.

Poor little church,
tossed about by the waves of a violent storm,
with no harbor of refuge.
Cast your cares on the Lord,
for He Himself will help you
nourishing you at the fountain of your princes, the Apostles.
They were fortified with the teachings of Christ,
and the grace of the Holy Spirit;
draw strength from them
from then until now,
so that growing from virtue to virtue
you will be able to see the God of gods in Zion
to whom be honor and glory throughout all ages. Amen.

(II/20)

21.

Lord Jesus Christ,
we thank you
for you have deigned
to accept as the first fruits of faith
the gifts of your people,
whom you have established as your Church.
To you be honor and glory
through eternal ages. Amen.

(III/77)

The people of God
have journeyed from
the earthly city
to the heavenly
Jerusalem.
Giusto
de' Menabuoi,
*St. Anthony
announces the
liberation of Padua*
(detail) Basilica of
St. Anthony.

22.

Christ Jesus,
you conquered the pride of the evil one
by the humility of your incarnation:
grant also to us
to shatter the chains of pride and arrogance
by the humility of our heart,
so that we may be worthy of the gift of your glory.
With your help
who are blessed from age to age. Amen.

(I/145)

With the humility
of his incarnation
Jesus has defeated
the rebellion
against God.
Altichiero da Zevio
*Presentation in the
Temple* (detail)
Chapel
of St. George.

47

SAINT ANTHONY PRAYS TO THE HOLY SPIRIT

1.

Holy Spirit, fire of love,
come rest over each of us,
make our tongue ready to confess our sins,
that in revealing everything and concealing nothing,
we may attain heavenly life
to sing eternal praise with the angels.
With your help,
you who live and reign through all ages. Amen.

(I/381)

2.

Holy Spirit,
you who are the love of the Father and the Son,
let your love cover the multitude of our sins.
To you be honor and glory
throughout all ages. Amen.

(I/364)

The Holy Spirit
cleanses us and
makes us worthy of
eternal life.
Altichiero da Zevio
Coronation of Mary
(detail) Chapel of
St. George.

3.

We beg you, Holy Spirit,
pour out the salve of your mercy
like the good samaritan
on the wounds of our soul.
Bind them with the bandages of your grace,
mount our souls on the pack animal of obedience,
lead it to the shelter of conversion:
entrust us to the care of contrition of the soul,
so that we may rest under your care for a long time,
until we recover our lost salvation
with the money of true repentance.
After having found it,
grant that we may have the strength
to return on the road which leads to you
from which we strayed.
With your help
you who reign with the Father and the Son
for all ages. Amen.

(II/191)

St. Anthony brings
the mercy of God
among men which
heals divisions
among them.
Titian, *Miracle
of the Infant,*
School of the Saint.

4.

With humility and devotion
O Holy Spirit,
we ask you to pour out your grace upon us,
so we can celebrate the feast of the Spirit
by keeping your commandments
and mortifying our senses.
Fill us with sincere sorrow
kindle over us the light of your presence,
so in your radiance we can see almighty God
in the splendor of your saints.
With your help
you who are one God in three,
blessed throughout all ages. Amen.

(I/385)

The Spirit of God
has made
St. Anthony
a glorious witness
of the faith.

Girolamo Tessari,
*The miracle of the
donkey adoring the
Eucharist* (detail)
School of the Saint.

SAINT ANTHONY PRAYS TO THE BLESSED VIRGIN MARY

1.

We beg you,
our Lady and our hope,
you, who are the star of the sea,
illumine your children,
engulfed in the turbulent sea of sin;
guide us to the safe harbor of forgiveness,
so we may successfully complete the journey of our life
with your protection.
With his help
whom you carried in your womb,
and nourished at your holy breasts.
To him be honor and glory
throughout all ages. Amen.

(I/163)

The Mother of Jesus is the star which guides us to a safe harbor.
Altichiero da Zevio, *Adoration of the Magi* (detail) Chapel of St. George.

2.

We ask you, Our Lady,
you who are called the morning star,
dispel with your light
the thick fog of allurements to evil
which fills our souls.
Like the light of the moon,
replenish our emptiness,
and dissipate the darkness of our sins,
so that we may attain the fullness of eternal life
and the light of never diminishing glory.
With his help, who made you our light,
and although born from you,
gave you life.
To him be honor and glory
from age to age. Amen.

(II/108)

The glory of Mary
is the hope of
eternal life for
her children.
Altichiero da Zevio,
Coronation of Mary
(detail) Chapel of
St. George.

3.

Our Lady,
our only hope,
we are asking you to illumine our souls
with the brilliance of your grace,
to cleanse us with the splendor of your purity,
to cheer us with the warmth of your presence,
and to reconcile us to your Son,
that we may be worthy of his glory.
With his help
who assumed his glorious flesh from you,
and who wished to live in your womb for nine months.
To him be honor and glory
through all eternity. Amen.

(II/114)

Mary under the
cross of Jesus
helped with the
reconciliation of
all people.
Altichiero da Zevio,
Crucifixion (detail)
Chapel of St.
George.

59

4.

Lady and Mother of God,
your name is like a fortified tower
in which every sinner finds refuge and salvation.
O sweet name,
a name which comforts sinners.
O name of blessed hope.
You, O Virgin, are in the recesses of the soul.
Your name is like a shining light,
Like a sweet taste in the mouth,
Like a delightful song in the ears of your children.

(I/162)

5.

O Mary,
you are a throne
in which is located the glory of the Father.
On this throne Jesus Christ, true Wisdom,
took his place,
Glory Itself, greater than any of the angels,
who lived on the earth in our flesh.
You, blessed Mary,
became the seat of that Glory, Jesus Christ,
to whom be honor and praise from age to age. Amen.

(II/141)

St. Anthony is for
us an example of
faith and prayer.
Titian, *Miracle
of the foot*
(detail) School of
the Saint.

INDEX

Finito di stampare 1986
Editrice - Grafiche Messaggero di S. Antonio, Padova